For Melanie Pirotta – S.G.

For Nick, Cathryn and Steven, with love – S.A.

Text copyright © 2002 Sam Godwin
Illustrations copyright © 2002 Simone Abel
Volume copyright © 2002 Hodder Wayland

Series concept and design: Liz Black
Book design: Jane Hawkins
Editor: Katie Orchard
Science Consultant: Dr Carol Ballard

Published in Great Britain in 2002 by Hodder Wayland,
an imprint of Hodder Children's Books
Reprinted in 2003

Cataloguing in publication data
Godwin, Sam
  All Kinds of Everything: a first look at materials. – (Little Bees)
  1. Materials – Pictorial works – Juvenile literature
  I. Title
620.1'1

ISBN 07502 3933 6

Printed and bound in Grafiasa, Portugal

Hodder Children's Books
A division of Hodder Headline Limited
338 Euston Road, London NW1 3BH

All Kinds of Everything

A first look at materials

All Kinds of Everything
A first look at materials

Sam Godwin

HODDER
Wayland

an imprint of Hodder Children's Books

Everything around us is

Ow! I didn't see that coming!

It's made of glass, Titch. You can see through it, but it's a solid material.

6

made of different materials.

Hey, this window's open! Let's go in.

Some materials are made by people.

Look at all these things, Zip. Some are shiny, some are rough...

8

Materials can be solid or liquid.

My web is soft and bendy, just like jelly!

Hey, Zip, can you stretch everything like jelly?

No, Titch. Some hard materials, like glass, can't stretch.

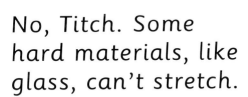

There are hard solids and soft ones.

11

Liquids flow freely, like water.

Materials change when they become hot.

Oh, no! I'm getting wet!

Water becomes steam.

Steam changes back into water when it cools down.

I hope that chocolate doesn't change into anything else before I get there!

17

21

Liquids turn into solids when they become cold.

Water freezes and turns into ice.

The warm orange juice will melt the ice.

It takes all kinds of materials to make up a world.

Wow! It looks like all those materials have turned into a party!

28

All about materials

We use lots of different materials every day, such as wood, paper, metal, plastic, glass, sand, stone, wool or cloth.

Some materials are natural and some are made by people.

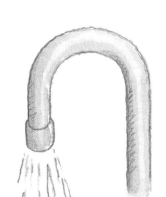

Solids can be hard or soft.

Materials can be solid or liquid.

You can pour some liquids into some solid objects.

Some materials melt when they become hot.

Liquids *freeze* when they become cold.

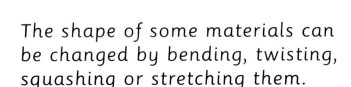

The shape of some materials can be changed by bending, twisting, squashing or stretching them.

Useful Words

Dissolve
When a solid, such as sugar, disapppears into a liquid, such as water.

Freeze
When a liquid becomes so cold it turns into a solid. Water becomes ice when it freezes.

Melt
When a solid, such as jelly, is heated and turns into a liquid.

Transparent
See-through.

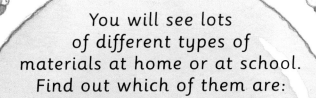

You will see lots of different types of materials at home or at school. Find out which of them are:

warm   squashy   shiny   cold

stretchy   transparent   magnetic

hard   bendy   wobbly   rough

twisty   smooth   bendy   soft

able to float   hot   dull